The Qualified Life

Veonne Anderson

The Qualified Life

ISBN: 978-0-578-73657-0 (Paperback)

Printed by Written Legacy, Inc.

Written Legacy, Inc.
5878 Covington Hwy, Box 03
Decatur, GA, 30035

www.VeonneAnderson.com

9780578736570

For Someone Special:

On this date, ____/____/_____, I am gifting this book to

_____

because I believe that you have great potential and a life that is

destined for greatness.

The Qualified Life

Table of Contents

This book is dedicated to some of the most important people in my life.

My daughter Joii: Thank you for being the light that you are. Your smile has helped me press through the roughest times in mommy's journey. I love you beyond words. Thank you for giving mommy life and hope. I love you beyond the moon.

My mom: You are strong, you are wonderfully made. Thank you for your phone calls and encouragement to go for the best things in life. Thank you for believing in me, thank you for your laughs and thank you for your cheer leading for me even in the trenches. I love you.

My grandmother: Gigi, thank you for seeing the best in me from the beginning. Thank you for your love. Thank you for being my cheerleader - even when I didn't feel qualified to be recognized. Thank you for all the times you said, "my granddaughter's a Motivational Author" when I didn't have the faith to write books like this again. I love you.

To Janet Lake & Erica Rooks: Thank you for being in my life in the darkest time of my life. Thank you for your encouragement, random times of picking me up and taking me out to lunch just to talk. Thank you for tearing down my walls (gracefully) and thank you for building me up. Thank you for not abandoning me when I wanted to give up in my faith walk. Thank you for seeing beyond my pain and seeing the TRUE person God made me to be. Thank you for your unconditional love, you both mean more to me than you could ever imagine. God used both of you to save my life when I didn't believe there was life beyond my hurt. I love you both.

The Qualified Life

Prelude

When God told me to write The Qualified Life, I thought to myself... I'm not even qualified to write this book! What a coincidence, right? At the moment (May 2017), I am living with my husband's grandparents, bankrupt and living off food stamps. As I update July 9, 2019, I am going through a divorce to the man I dedicated my whole life to. March 22, 2020, I am living in Georgia, writing on my new computer, in the midst of the Coronavirus pandemic, living a new life. June 14, 2020, I have successfully finished my edits and have seen TREMENDOUS growth in my life - it's like I'm a completely different, transformed woman.

The Qualified Life

My life spiraled so fast 2 years ago, I didn't know how to recover. I felt like I would never smile again. To have joy again seemed so far-fetched. But God is a redeemer of time! He is The Healer of all hearts looking for healing. I had to give God my "yes" again…because the beginning of my divorce process almost took me OUT. I was mentally drained, spiritually depleted and I felt like giving up on the God that loved me at my worst. He picked me up again, and put me back on track - and for that, I am thankful. It's like my life had been through the Job experience. The worst of my life turned out to make a better version of my life than I could have never expected. The ugly can reshape your life into a beautiful restoration - like a butterfly in a cocoon.

Life made me spiral into a deep depression a few years ago to the point I put this book down for two years because I felt like my life was going through hell. Then, I felt the leading of God to write again. Imagine, God telling you to pick this book back up to continue writing while going through everything that disqualifies you to talk about being qualified for anything. Who am I to write about being qualified?! Especially after being a backslider that went to school for ministry - phew. This call was making me really walk by faith.

I found it absurd that God would have me pick this book back up. Going through divorce while also processing all the losses I've experienced has been a tough one. As I pick this book back up, I am reminded that it's not about what you are going through that makes you qualified - it's about God's hand positioning you to be Qualified. If there was any time that I felt qualified, it was in my successes in the past. I was making a good amount of money at my job in sales, I had an AMAZING sports car and I had my own everything. To man, this would qualify me – but God chose me to write about being qualified in one of the lowest moments of my life.

It is in this season of my life that God has taken me through the process of humility, honesty and honing the ugly about me that He wanted to change in my life. God has been revealing to me that

The Qualified Life

He is the one that has qualified me. Qualification isn't based on my Earthly qualifications. Yes, my college degree is good. My qualification in graphic design and publishing books is great. My expertise in business branding is awesome. Yes, I saved my virginity until I was married - but now that's irrelevant. The very thing I considered making me the most significant person in the room is now gone. EVERY qualification that I gave myself - gone. However, God had a bigger destiny and qualification in store – but it began with humility.

"The LORD doesn't see things the way you see them. People judge by outward appearance, but the LORD looks at the heart." 1 Samuel 16:7 (NLT)

I am now in the place where I am officially starting over and resting in God's approval - not man's. It all begins with deleting all 7 books I've written, being divorced and allowing God to be the one to qualify me. It's easy to write books on things that you've experienced and/or have knowledge in, without the guidance of God. This is the time when I am starting fresh - from a place of understanding and compassion. A part of me experiencing the true Qualified Life is allowing God to build and establish my foundation - without me getting it done with the typical churchy qualifications.

I have learned in the past few years the power of letting go of the past in order to take hold of the new things that God has in store. Some time ago, I would use my past accomplishments as a means of me being qualified to do something, however I was broken and truly had nothing to boast about. However, I have been humbled by the Lord Almighty, and I now commit my endeavors to Him. No longer will I try to make my own way nor exalt myself to be "qualified", but I now stand on the principles in this book to walk in The Qualified Life.

As you read this book, I pray that the Lord ministers to you and helps you understand who you truly are in Him. I pray that depression and confusion about your identity will leave you as you read these truths, and that the grace of God would transform your life forever. I pray that you will see that you truly are qualified to walk in God's calling for your life. May this book bless you, educate you and heal your bruises from negative words spoken over your destiny. And may the shackles of poverty leave your mind, no longer having power over your life.

Be Great,

Veonne Anderson

Introduction

From the beginning of time, mankind has been challenged with the thought of not being good enough, not measuring up, not being qualified enough to achieve greatness. We live in a time where being relevant can change in an instant if you are not famous on social media - where your fashion must make a statement to be considered worthy in order to be heard. The culture that we live in exalts talent; and if you are not branded and talented enough – you most likely won't be successful.

But what happens if an individual hasn't identified their talent? Where do the people that haven't tapped into their full potential, run to? Are they supposed to sit on the sidelines and watch everyone run the rat race to fame and success? I believe that there are over 80% of people in this world that don't know their God-given purpose. There are billions of people on this Earth that have no clue the limit of their

potential, their talents, their capacity and even their purpose.

This book has been tailor made to open your eyes concerning your

potential. You will finally discover that no matter what has been told

to you – from family, friends, teachers, exes, culture, etc. - you are

good enough. The odds were meant to turn around in your favor –

but now will be the time that you will finally see that you were born

for greatness. If your adversaries thought they could kill you –

they're going to be sorry they didn't do it a long time ago.

By the end of this book – you will be equipped with the weapon of

knowledge to destroy every lie and every word that has been formed

to water down your true identity.

By the end of this book, you will finally discover that no matter what you have gone through in the past nor what you may be going through at the moment...

You are qualified.

The Qualified Life

Chapter 1: Who You Are vs. What You Do

""Before I formed you in the womb, I knew you.

Before you were born, I set you apart for my holy

purpose. I appointed you to be a prophet to the

nations." Jeremiah 1:5 (GWT)

Have you ever felt as though you had no purpose in this life? Have you ever had a very tough situation going on in your life to the point where it seemed that your life wasn't worth living? I have. There was a moment in my life in 2011 where I felt that God was disappointed in my disobedience to Him that I was on the verge of committing suicide. I got into my car one day and I heard in my head, "You should just run your car off the road". At that moment, I felt like I disappointed God. I crank up the car and began to drive.

When I began driving out of my neighborhood, I heard the voice of God say, "Turn the car around and go home". There was so much authority and strength in this voice. I immediately obeyed. I was in such a dark and low place, but God's arm was not too short or far away to rescue me and pull me out from my dark place. As soon as I got into my driveway, I began to weep and cry out to God. It was that day that I broke off the relationship with my then boyfriend. We were not in any type of sexual sin, but God told me that he was not my husband and I needed to break it off. After I did it, I felt a weight come off of my soul.

Your freedom is dependent upon your obedience.

Fast forward to 2019 - dealing with the shame of going through a divorce had me question my purpose in life. I had my life mapped out on what my future would be and to have that end, I felt like I failed. I constantly questioned if I was strong enough to start my life over. Would I ever love again? Could I be a good example of a mother to my daughter as I struggled to get my feet replanted in Georgia? My life was accustomed to making a certain amount of money, and I had to start over making minimum wage.

God knew that it was going to be a temporary situation, but I couldn't see beyond the circumstance I was dealing with in that moment of time. I felt desperate, like a failure and ultimately - I felt alone. It didn't make me any better having a family member tell me that it seemed like I was trying to make up for lost time, and not doing enough (because I didn't have a job). I knew that was the complete opposite because I was bustin' my butt to provide for my daughter and myself. I had to make things work with $200 a month, then I got hired to be a theater teacher to then find out I was being let go due to budget cuts, to then having to work at the airport to make ends meet.

Sometimes you'll go through things that people don't understand. Your process won't be understood by all, and that's okay. You have to know the truth about yourself, self evaluate and develop a plan to get where you need to go in life. If I would have accepted what that person said and what my family thought of me, I wouldn't have completed this book. Behind the scenes, I was completing The Qualified Life, creating websites for people and pushing my vision beyond where I currently was. I was in a building state - but not everyone was able to see the blueprint - they only saw the incomplete construction on the outside. I had to be sober minded, which meant I could not let their words replay in my mind.

"Be alert and of sober mind. Your enemy the devil prowls around like a roaring lion looking for someone to devour." 1 Peter 5:8 (NIV)

The enemy wanted to take me out. He waits patiently for the opportune moment to attack someone. It starts with small thoughts, in the midst of a hard and low moment, that's when the real attack comes. Every moment that seems like opposition are seeds that the enemy plants to lead up to his ultimate attack which has a destiny defining moment. You must be wise to see when God has a moment in time for you to choose where your life can have a destiny defining shift - your destiny is hanging in the balance.

There were days where I isolated myself, and there were days that I felt heavy from burdens or shame from not fulfilling something that I committed I would do for the Lord. I carried so much condemnation, my religious mindset seemed to have held me in periods of depression because I thought religion meant that I had to be perfect. This is not God's will for your faith. Jesus said that He came to give you LIFE AND ABUNDANT LIFE! If your religion is a burden, you must evaluate if you are living your faith based upon works you do or if you are actually living by faith that the Lord designed for you to have. Are you living by condemnation or false religious hype?

What I want you to know is that God has a purpose for your life. Jeremiah 1:5 lets you know that God has a purpose for your life. Before you were born – God set you apart and had a specific plan for you. He set you apart for a holy purpose. When saying this – it doesn't mean that you were called to be a pastor or a preacher.

The Qualified Life

JEREMIAH was called to be a prophet to the nations. YOU are not Jeremiah.

You must discover from your Creator who you were fashioned and formed to be in this earth. God gives us the ability to prophesy when we are living a life that is set apart for the work of the Lord - I've even seen Him use people when they aren't living for Him. God wants you to prophecy! Don't believe me?

"Let love be your highest goal! But you should also desire the special abilities the Spirit gives--especially the ability to prophesy."

1 Corinthians 14:1 (NLT)

As I was saying, Jeremiah was called to the office of a prophet – because that's what God made and called him to be. It is up to us to get into a relationship with God, meaning connect with God on a personal level, and get to know what we are called to be. What is it that God has called you to do? If you don't know what God is calling you to do, it is not too late! That is why God put it on your heart to read this book.

Over a series of years I found myself signing up for multiple commitments, side hustles to make money and chasing career paths that I was not designed to do – and I was burnt out! But it wasn't until I sat down with God and I asked Him specifically what He wanted me to do with my life that I found peace and a pathway on which path my life should go.

Everyone around you and even those that you have not met yet are affected by your decisions. **Your destiny is connected to people, places and decisions.** If you are not in sync with your destiny and doing activities that place you in position for your purpose in life, you will find that you are draining your energy, hanging with the wrong people and you are also delaying the freedom of the people you are called to reach in the world.

And another thing…we weren't called to reach EVERY SINGLE PERSON in the world. God has called you to a specific group of people. A particular people are called to follow the direction of your leadership. As believers, we are called by God to disciple others - which is defined as "to teach and instruct". You aren't called to disciple everyone - because Jesus also lets us know in John 4:37 that some plant the seed and another will see the harvest of the planting. 1 Corinthians 3:6 says it great as well, "I planted the seed, Apollos watered it, but God has been making it grow. So neither the one who plants nor the one who waters is anything, but only God, who makes things grow. The one who plants and the one who waters have one purpose, and they will each be rewarded according to their own labor. For we are co-workers in God's service; you are God's field, God's building." So, you can take that extra pressure off of you to save everybody. You'll burn out, quick, trying to reap a harvest that isn't your garden to tend to.

If you are not on the path to the right purpose, those people that you are called to are delayed in meeting with THEIR destiny moment – because you were called to position them. Jeremiah was called to the nations – but God revealed "the nations" to him as a part of the revelation of his destiny. It requires for you to be connected to God to know the people that you are called to. God wants you to connect with Him for more details instead of you trying to figure it out on your own.

Have you ever heard the story of Joseph in the bible? Joseph had dreams from God that he would rule over people one day - he knew from childhood that he was born to be a leader. His position did not come in the way that he thought it would, but he knew from God that he was called to leadership. God called him to the leadership role to save his nation and his people - it wasn't just to make Joseph a great man. You are called to greatness to build people - not your ego. It's never just about you.

Honestly, I was that type of person that would try to use my own understanding of putting the puzzle pieces together. But God is a complex Being. What makes sense to YOU is completely opposite of what God wants to do in your life. I had an idea of what my life's purpose would be…and God flipped that thing upside down like the

The Qualified Life

Fresh Prince[1]. Proverbs 3:5 says it best – don't lean to your own understanding. Acknowledge God in *all* of your ways because He is the one that will direct your path.

When I began writing this book in May 2017, I thought I finally had it all together. But the trials following led me to a greater depth of knowing Him and gave me more understanding to what living in grace really meant. It was after everything began to fall apart: my marriage, my sense of direction and my plan for my life, where I really found God. I found God in my darkest moment - how? He is The Light! You're looking for "something" in your darkest moments - and that thing that you're looking for is light. The only "light" is Jesus and He is Salvation! HE is your Rescue! You think you're looking for answers, but HE is your ANSWER!

Now, I have clarity, direction and a purpose that is totally worth living for, because I live in His grace and His love. He qualified me in my lowest. He gave me understanding in the time of my life where

---

[1] Fresh Prince Of Bel-air. Television show.

everything seemed hectic. But baby, I'm called and I'm qualified...and I don't care what you say about me! I'm officially a dangerous woman because I gave God my, YES!

Have you given God the keys over the journey regarding your life's journey? Can you really say that you can trust Him, with your life? When you recognize that you are in the hands of God, you officially become a dangerous weapon. Why? When you are in the leading of God's instruction, you can never go wrong! He has the bird's eye view of your destiny; He sees the beginning and the end all in one. He knows you and wouldn't put you in a place where you are destined to fail. Even if it *seems* like a fail in your eyes, God has a greater understanding of what is going on than you can comprehend. It's like those moments where you look back and you say, "wow, now I understand why I had to go through that!" His word promises us that *all things work together for the good of those who love Him.*

God would never make you fail - with His direction, because He wants the glory for **all** of your successes. If it seems like you have failed, think of it this way, sometimes your "failures" are life lessons. Some of your greatest failures are your best lessons in life. Maybe you found yourself in some regretful moments because you decided to follow your own path and not God's perfect will - God will use it as a key of wisdom to unlock doors of opportunity for you. Trust me, I know all about that. If I had allowed God's timing to perfect what He desired to do in my life in certain times in my life, I would have avoided many troubles. But I can honestly say that those failures made me realize just how merciful He is. Not only that, but I've also learned great wisdom which helped me to know how to navigate life better and avoid the obstacles that I would easily fall into in the past.

You are not a failure, your obstacles will soon be a road map for others to gain wisdom from. Your story is full of experiences, and no one is allowed to disqualify you from your experiences - it's what makes you unique. But, are you willing to truly be who God wants you to be? Who God wants you to be is, the true you. You are not who you think you were made to be from opinions of people or your talents/gifts. Your limitations are only deciding to operating in your own understanding

Only God can define you and give you true language for who you really are. People may think that they know who you are, but they have no idea how great the plans are that God has in store for you. Colossians 3:1-4 tells us to *put on the new self.* Your true identity and definition of who you are is hidden in God; and the only way to know who we are is through discovering Him.

Notes

Chapter 2: Where Did Your Doubt Begin?

Have you ever been told that you were not capable of being the person that you always felt that you were made to be? I remember being a teenager on the crossroads of what my career choice would be; I had the choice of being an artist, actress or something that I didn't really care about. I loved acting but my passion at that time was drawing. Not being biased, but I was an amazing artist! Well, I remember someone who had a big influence in my life at the time telling me that being an artist wouldn't make me any money and I needed to take another career. I took that person's advice. Why in the world did I listen?! I have no idea. But what I do know was that my hope was crushed.

I began looking at other options for my future career and considered the military. But when I took the ASVAB test for the military, the results shocked me. Apparently, I was only equipped to work in the cafeteria. What in the world?! There's absolutely nothing wrong with being a cafeteria worker; in school I had such a love for them since they were often not acknowledged. I've met some of the greatest people that worked in the cafeteria... but the government misidentified my purpose in life. If I had listened to what the military tests chose for my destiny rather than finding my identity in God and also identifying my gifts, I wouldn't be writing this book today. My destiny was bigger than what anyone could suggest or assume what my future would be. What if I listened to them and worked in the cafeteria because they told me that's all I was good for?

So again, my question is, who told you that you can't do something? What is that one thing that you dreamed of doing but you allowed a person to stop you from pursuing it? The reason that people have the ability to make us lose faith in our dreams is only because they were not created to carry it, therefore they have the potential to sabotage it. People who lack vision will never have the vision that you have to live out your dream. Why? It's YOUR dream.

The beautiful thing about the Qualified life is that there will always be someone out there who will believe in your vision, so they can be a part of it. Believe it or not, there are people out there that can and will support you; but if you don't have the vision written down - no one can run with it (Habakkuk 2:2). How could a building ever be built without a blueprint? The same applies to your ideas and visions - no one can build where there is no plan for them to review.

If you had an idea to create something, and you decide to go on TV to pitch your business idea, do you truly believe that if you have no idea structured on paper, with numbers and goals...that they'd invest in your idea? Absolutely not. No millionaire, billionaire or trillionaire would invest in anything that is not written. Writing on paper is a legal document. And if you have nothing written - it will not become a reality - an illegal dream. Writing makes something legal.

Protecting Your Vision

Protecting your vision is one of the most important keys to walking in the purpose that God had given you before the foundations of the earth. There's always going to be an adversary attempting to steal your vision or fight against your "it". Why?

"Where there is no vision, the people perish: but he that keepeth the law, happy is he." Proverbs 29:18 (KJV)

The devil knows that if he can steal your vision, you will perish - die. You may not die physically, but you will die in your motivation. Have you not noticed from childhood how many people are discouraged to do the things that they loved? Take a step back and think about how many lives have had their innocence and/or imagination stolen from them in their time of growing up. When innocence is taken from a child, it taints their vision - their perspective of themselves. It causes confusion and confusion distorts the imagination. When the imagination is stolen, purpose feels out of reach.

There are also children that have had their dreams crushed after sharing with their family and/or peers about their passions. You'll often see these types of children acting out in class, unmotivated or suffering from an identity crisis because someone told them that their dreams were not able to be reached. Ask me how I know. I lived it. Most of my school career I acted out in school because my innocence was tainted, and I was distracted by the cares of life that were far beyond my control. You must protect your vision.

Visionless Bystanders

Many of us have had experiences where we have shared our vision with the wrong people, and one of 4 things have happened:

1.   They told you that the idea was not possible.

The Qualified Life

2.   They used your past against you to disqualify you from obtaining that vision.

3.   You discovered they were thieves; they took your idea and ran with it.

4.   They ignored you or downplayed your idea.

As creative, innovative people we must be sure not to share our best ideas with people who cannot comprehend what we have to offer the world. If someone has no vision to better their lives and cannot can't see beyond where they are now - they cannot value what you have to offer.

I began to notice this in my life when I would share big ideas with people that I thought would join me in rejoicing - but they responded, "oh, okay", or "that's far-fetched" - and they were right, it was far-fetched...for them. It wasn't their vision! You cannot share your vision with people that cannot carry it out for, and with you. There comes a point in your life where you have to dust the haters off and keep your focus on attaining destiny! Not everyone will be able to join and enjoy the ride to your success. Sometimes family will even be excluded from knowing what's going on with your vision - because they are too familiar with you and cannot see where God is taking you. But take heart beloved, your advancement is not in the hands of your enemies - it is in the hands of the Lord!

"All things are done according to God's plan and decision;..."

Ephesians 1:11 (Good News Translation)

"My times are in your hands..." Psalm 31:15 (NIV)

If you desire to live an abundant, joyful, successful life, you must understand that everything that pertains to your life is in the hands of the Lord. No hustle can get you where you NEED to be; God will position you. No demon in hell can take you out when you are in His perfect will. You have nothing to fear because everything is in God's hands.

The Qualified Life

"He controls the course of world events; he removes kings and sets up other kings. He gives wisdom to the wise and knowledge to the scholars." Daniel 2:21 (NLT)

Notes

The Qualified Life

Chapter 3: Take Over!

Imagine, you receive a letter in the mail telling you that you have been qualified to receive a FREE mega mansion. You probably wouldn't believe it, considering you get junk mail quite often. As you continue reading the letter, you read that the only thing that you need to do in order to get this FREE house would be to go learn about the history of the home from the past owner, their requirements for maintaining the house, get the deed paperwork filled out and simply go live in it.

Oh, and one more thing, your biggest mission involved in their request was to be an agent of "change" for the good of the neighborhood. This would be included but not limited to making sure the neighborhood had a cleaning crew, curfews, security and everything that would be needed for a safe, thriving neighborhood. Would you be willing to take on the responsibility for change? Does this change your decision because your responsibilities increased?

The Qualified Life

This illustration is made to show you the price of what we call OCCUPYING. Every human being on earth has been given a purpose and with that purpose, they were assigned a place to use their influence - the place they were created to occupy. If you desire to be a person of influence, you are going to have to OCCUPY a place for a specific time and people that need the change you have to offer.

Your Presence Is A Need

Where there is a need, there is a person that is not in their designated place to occupy. Where there is deserted space, there is abandonment of responsibility. There is nothing more tragic than an unoccupied piece of real estate. I hate seeing unoccupied buildings in the hood, why? It shows that there was once a small business there, streets where children used to play and history that has been visibly erased. It takes positioned people to prosper a land. And where there are no buyers, there is no thriving in a community. As people, we have the responsibility to take ownership of our responsibilities. Abandoned neighborhoods show the deficit of healthy families and healthy communities.

What Do You Own?

One of the greatest revelations that I received while writing this book is the revelation of ownership. I was laying down in my bed and I began to think about the value of land, in a way that I've never seen it before. I began to see within the vision of my mind that ownership of land and property is key to living a life of dominion.

You cannot rule over what you do not own.

What do you own? Do you own anything? If not, you rule nothing. What you do not own can be taken away from you. This is why it is so necessary that we get out of the mindset of renting properties and turn our focus towards ownership. Now, if you need to rent to build your credit, I can understand your goal. However, you must have the sole purpose of ownership, otherwise you are a slave to a system that wants to keep you in debt and dependent upon them. God wants you to own so you can live without the burdens of poverty. What is the difference between a slave and a master? Ownership of land. If a slave owns land, they are a slave to no one.

If you are planning to live a life of leadership and authority, you must think ownership. What are some habits in your life that you need to break in order to become an owner of property? How about...compulsive spending? Spending money on materials, junk food and random things will not give you the keys to ownership - pun intended. At the end of the chapter, write some action steps and things that need to change so you can own. If you own land/property, write action steps for your next lordship venture.

Keys

We have all been given keys to thrive in life, however we must know where those keys come from. Hidden within you are gifts/abilities to do something to make an impact in this world. However, if you don't connect with your "Locksmith", you will never access the keys to open the doors to your opportunities. Keys are for access to doors. Doors are ways of access to walk into a new realm of influence and networking. Without keys, you own nothing. When you are leasing, your keys can be taken away from you based upon the legal owner of the property. That is why it is important that you learn everything that you need to know in order to become the influence that you were created to be so your keys cannot be taken away from you.

Material things and relationships are temporary. Things fade and people die, it's a part of life; but knowledge & Wisdom are keys that cannot be taken away from you. What do you have keys to? What are the gifts that you have in you that are ready to be unlocked?

Ownership In Your Realm Of Influence

The truth of the matter is, not everyone is called to be the lead strategist for a fortune 500 company. Everyone in the world will not have a million dollars in their bank account at one time, not even six figures. However, we must know that there is wealth hidden within our abilities to make the most of our limitless opportunities. **We were all created with a capacity, a depth and ability to make an impact daily.** Each mission that we've been given is already mapped out for us, but until we get to know God on a relational level we will miss out on what our life is supposed to truly look like. Doesn't that kinda change the way that you think? Your life is already planned out.

"Your eyes saw my unformed body; all the days ordained for me were written in your book before one of them came to be."

Psalm 139:16 (NIV)

If you knew that your life was planned out, and that it could change for the better at any moment, how would your life be different from your current state of life? The problem is, we lean on our own understanding and we try to create a life that we fantasize about, or those we compare our lives to on social media. And the outrageous plot twist is that we were never intended to live out these unrealistic fantasies. Many of the fantasies that you have about your future are probably tailored around social media lifestyle photos, television/celebrities or someone that you've envied. Our life has been planned out by God, but we have gotten in the way of how the story is supposed to go. Some of the intense action that is going on in your life is supposed to take place. There is no good story without conflict! The beauty of conflict is the story of how you overcome the tribulations.

Something that you have to do is take ownership of your mission in life. Your mission is your calling. You may be in a conflict between choosing your own path and the path that has been ordained for you before you were born. While writing this book, I had to come to the understanding that God had given me a unique assignment in life to use my words to bring understanding and healing to people that felt broken. I thought this book was going one way, but then God made it clear to me that I had to be okay with the changes that He wanted to make.

You have to love who you were designed to be and who you were designed to reach.

Accepting your call isn't going to always feel like running through a field of daisies, it most likely will be what you least expected or a compilation of childhood passions you had; and that's okay. There was a time in my life where I wanted to run away from what God wanted me to do. I was a nice person, but I didn't like getting involved with people's "issues" - just being honest. I LOVE talking to people, but dealing with problems was another thing. But, to have that outlook on life is the complete opposite of what Jesus was like. I mean, didn't He take on all of our burdens? Isn't He involved in our lives? Take ownership of whatever your mission in life is and take pride that God entrusts you with something. You cannot gain access to true Godly success when you do not take ownership of what you've been given.

Here are some questions to take God regarding your life:

What is the realm of influence that I am made for?

Who are the people that I am designed to impact?

After finding that out, you must take ownership of your mission. How will that change your actions for your day-to-day routine?

What Am I To Be Occupying?

"And God blessed them, and God said unto them, Be fruitful, and multiply, and replenish the earth, and subdue it: and have dominion over the fish of the sea, and over the fowl of the air, and over every living thing that moveth upon the earth."

Genesis 1:28 (KJV)

The Qualified Life

God originally created mankind to do the following:

1. **Be Fruitful**

2. **Multiply**

3. **Replenish** The Earth

4. **Subdue** The Earth

5. **Have Dominion** over the fish of the sea, the birds of the air and over every living **thing** that moves upon the earth.

The first thing that I want to establish before I move forward into expounding on occupying is that God told man to have dominion over every living THING - not people. I want to highlight this because sometimes people take this verse, and they run into problems trying to run people and not THINGS. Your money is a thing, but the people who work for you are not to be dominated over - they are to be led.

Leading is not dominating people, these are two different actions. When people are led correctly, they are trained to one day do that what you do so that one day they can keep the legacy going. Leadership has a lasting legacy and growing generations in mind; dominators leave people in the condition of the 3 D's - *damaged*, *dependent* upon them and eventually *dead*. These are all characteristics of an abusive relationship - and the same applies for leaders leading in toxic relationships with disciples. When people dominate and occupy territories, you will eventually see people rise up in anarchy. Now, let's discuss what God intended for occupying in your purpose.

Being Fruitful

When God said, *be fruitful* in Genesis, the Hebrew translation, according to Strong's H6509 for fruitful is the verb, "*parah*" which is defined as, "*(be, cause to be, make) fruitful, grow, increase*". This can be defined as being fruitful in the term of being fruitful by bearing

The Qualified Life

children - but I want to go by the definition above. God has called us to grow and increase - but how?

From birth, you were given a gift, and that gift is to be cultivated through mentorship / discipleship, development of your skill through education and is to be tested through fire (also known as trials). For some, fire may be criticism, it may be circumstances and it may even be through the process of patience - allowing God to groom you. Oh, yeah…being fruitful is more than just developing in those areas, you've got to grow and mature your spirit (your inner man). Why? When we grow spiritually, we get to know God in another way. The same thing applies with children, as they grow up they grow to know their parents in a more mature way - allowing room for growth and mature trust. God has given us a list of character traits that He wants to us to develop and He wants us to constantly grow in these area - the fruits of the Spirit.

"But the fruit of the Spirit is love, joy, peace, long suffering, gentleness, goodness, faith, meekness, temperance: against such there is no law."

Galatians 5:22-23 (KJV)

Have you grown in the fruits of the Spirit, or are you only desiring to be fruitful in your talents, gifts and or business? You cannot have a successful legacy in the Kingdom of God without the fruit of the Spirit to bear witness of what God has and is doing in your life. You may have done many things on the earth, but if you do not have love, which is the greatest commandment (Matthew 22:36-37) and all the other fruits of the spirit: joy, peace, long suffering, gentleness, goodness, faith, meekness and temperance - you have achieved nothing. What type of fruit have you been producing in your life? Is it something that God would be pleased with? Anything that is not of Him will not bear good fruit; and if something isn't bearing good fruit...I'll let you read it on the next page.

"A good tree cannot bear bad fruit, and a bad tree cannot bear good fruit. Every tree that does not bear good fruit is cut down and thrown into the fire. Thus, by their fruit you will recognize them."

Matthew 7:18-20 (NIV)

Multiply

According to Strong's Concordance H7235, the transliteration of multiply is the verb word, rabah, which has one of the definitions,

"to become many, become numerous, multiply (of people, animals, things)". Many times, we have great ideas and even words of encouragement that we keep to ourselves and never share with the world. It would be a shame to keep away something that was never meant to be kept to ourselves. Imagine, if Martin Luther King Jr., never had the boldness to speak for what he believed - where would the world be today? It takes faith to believe that what you have inside of you has the potential of being multiplied. The fruitfulness that

God wants you to produce is multiplication. What God expects from your life is the expansion and legacy of what He placed in you. Is your gift able to be multiplied, taught to the next generation to expand upon? Have you studied and cultivated what is in you so that others may reap the harvest of a greater future...and better yet, experience God?

We were created to be problem solvers.

There would be no need for multiplication if there was no lack or problems to be solved. I believe that America is in the recession that it is in today is simply because what was meant to be multiplied, has been selfishly handled. We are created to be problem solvers. God has given us the power to create wealth, therefore, if we can come together to make the change - we can. What resources do you have, or can use to solve problems you've felt compelled to change?

The Qualified Life

Where there is a problem, there is a person born to create the solution. This is the heart and character of God. In His presence, all problems are solved. Every problem requires faith in order to be solved, and multiplication can only be accessed through faith; *and without faith, it is impossible to please God.* (Hebrews 11:6, NIV) Without God, problems can't be solved.

I watched a documentary about the ecosystem and how water is constantly being moved throughout the Earth - water that we can't even see. When birds fly south for the winter, water get transported from their wings and waters the seeds in the land. The land feeds animals and animals fertilize the Earth (not to mention, they feed us too). I've always wondered, how do birds know when to fly? The documentary taught me that there is a change within the atmosphere (caused by water) and the birds respond to the shift in the water molecules in the air. Although we can't see the molecules with our eyes, the birds literally follow the water molecules to the south where it's warmer and to the place where water is! But who causes the shift?

Who commands the waters to tremble and leads the birds to their resources? GOD! He solved so many problems in that one scenario - and without that entire process, we would not have water. Surprisingly, this process even affects the rainforest - that's a whole other problem that needs to be solved. God is the greatest problem solver there is.

Lastly, God wants to multiply His image and likeness upon the earth. If God is seen in everything that we say and everything that we do, He will be exalted. 2 Corinthians 10:31 in the New International Version tells us, *"Whether therefore you eat, or drink, or whatsoever you do, do all to the glory of God."* Everything that we do, must be to glorify God. This means to put away your selfish desires, your plans, your agenda and all in order to allow Him to get the glory out of every part of your life SO THAT you may be fruitful.

Replenish The Earth

Male', the transliteration for replenish, means *"to fill, to be full, to accomplish, abundance, to satisfy"*. What I love about this word is that not only is it a verb, but it is a state of being. I love that the word replenish lets me know that God wants me to be filled, to live in abundance, to be satisfied and accomplished! This charge from God, considering grammatically,it is a verb, goes against the mentality that we are destined to live in poverty. God let us know, from the beginning that His original intent for our lives was abundance and success.

Therefore, you are QUALIFIED to live a life that is far beyond measure, because abundance has no limit. Why? Because once you hit one level of being filled, God wants to fill you AGAIN with more! You should never be satisfied with "just enough" because His word tells you that He wants to bless you to constantly be filled. Once you accomplish one measurement, it's time to go to the next level because your "fill" will always be challenged to go into a deeper depth than before.

Are you satisfied with where you are? If so, it is time to ask God to take your faith to the next dimension. Allow God to constantly stretch your faith so it is the lifestyle which you live by.

"For in it the righteousness of God is revealed from faith for faith, as it is written, "The righteous shall live by faith." Romans 1:17 (ESV)

There are many areas and problems within the earth that need to be filled. What is God telling you to replenish? What does God want you to fill? In order for us to know what needs to be filled, we need to ask God for His vision. You may think that you see a need, but God may be assigning you to do something there and more. His vision is always bigger than yours.

Fill empty places that need to be filled with God, hope and resources.

Subdue The Earth

When I began to read on the subject of subduing, I saw that the transliteration for the word was *"kabash"* which means *to subject, bring into bondage, keep under, force"*. I thought to myself, what does this have to do with living the Qualified life? But then, as I began to listen to the Lord, and He began to reveal to me that there will always be something within the earth that opposes the purpose that He has in store for you to do on the earth. It is our duty to make sure that we fulfill that purpose, even if it means that we get forceful, bring demonic forces into subjection by reinstating the law of the land - which is the Word of God. It means that there are going to be moments that you will have to put things under submission, spiritually.

Jesus told us in Matthew 16:19 (KJV), *"And I will give unto thee the keys of the kingdom of heaven: and whatsoever thou shalt bind on earth shall be bound in heaven: and whatsoever thou shalt loose on earth shall be loosed in heaven."*

So in other words, whatever you permit on earth is permitted in heaven, whatever is forbidden on earth, it is forbidden in heaven, God knew from the beginning that there would be spiritual warfare and mental battles in our lives, but He gave us authority through Jesus Christ by giving us the keys to the Kingdom. I mean, He does let us know that the Kingdom of God is in us (Luke 17:21) and the Kingdom is at hand (Matthew 3:2). Everything that we need is within us, but we can only access that through repentance, becoming one with Jesus and the perfect will of the Father.

Have Dominion

As I have mentioned before, dominion is not to be over people - God gave mankind specific instructions. Mankind was given *dominion over the birds of the air, the fish of the sea, and over every living thing that moves upon the earth.* This is why we find war in the land because there are people who want to rule people - which is against God's original intent. However, when God gives territory / land to someone, that land comes with provision: animals and resources. Why do you think it was so important for Adam and Eve to multiply and subdue the earth? God wanted to expand His dominion and glory throughout the entire earth, but Adam and Eve sinned in the garden and didn't have the vision to go beyond the garden. They were focused on what was before them and not what could possibly be on the other side of the garden.

God gave mankind dominion over the creatures, but have you ever thought that if He gave dominion over the creatures, that their territory would also be given along with them? How can you own something and not the habitat that keeps the thing sustained/living? Therefore, God gave man rulership over **the air** that the birds flew in, **the sea** the fish swam in, **the ground** that every animal and plant that was upon the earth. However, it must be taken care of, it had to be sustained and cultivated.

When it comes to your purpose, what has God given you dominion over? What territory have you been called to? Every territory has a language, culture and laws. There are people that you have been called to bring hope and life to, but you must understand that you must create a place (habitat) for God to have His way in, so these people can thrive there. God wants you to bring the dominion of the Kingdom into the places that some people are afraid to go. These places are where the lost are, but in order to win them, you must be set free from everything that keeps you in sin. You must be positioned to bring the Kingdom of God on earth.

With that being said, God has qualified you from the times before time existed. You've been given a mandate and charge from God to be fruitful, to multiply, replenish, subdue and dominate in your lifetime. You aren't meant to sit and live a normal life; The Qualified life is far from normal life - it calls you out of your comfort zone so you can bring change into the lives of the people God calls you to. You were created to be limitless in your realm of influence. (Ps. 82:6) Who told you that you weren't?

"I say, 'You are gods; you are all children of the Most High."

Psalm 82:6 (NLT)

We are not gods to be worshiped, but we are gods - God's children and therefore, since we are made in His image and likeness (Genesis 1:26, 27), we are gods. We have dominion over the things of this earth (Genesis 1:28). The question is, why have you been living less than the reflection of God that you were made to be? I dare to even ask, why are you living lesser than the god you were called in Psalm 82?

Notes

The Qualified Life

Chapter 4: Did He Really Say?

I remember the times in my childhood when I would hang out with my friends at the big, green electric transformer box in the neighborhood. I would get off the bus around 4 p.m., go inside the house to go grab a nice cheesy bag of Doritos with a Capri Sun and then I'd go find out if my friends were able to come out and play. These were the good old days – the days that neighbors knew their neighbors and everything was just good.

I don't know if you did this but, do you remember when you wanted to hang out at a friend's house and you put THEM on the phone to ask YOUR mom if YOU could spend the night? Yeah, I did. For some reason, we were really convinced if someone asked our parents for permission, our parents would magically change their minds. But if your parents said no, what were you to do about that? Either rebel against them or submit.

Well me, I was that kid that was free minded – doing what I wanted to do. So, words like "did she really say you can't do that?" would push me to do the complete opposite of what my superiors told me to do. There are people in this world that are manipulators and know the power of reverse psychology. I didn't realize how many manipulators I had in my life until I got in my adult years and looked back to my childhood and high school years. I was surrounded by SERPENTS!

Snake Bitten

We should always beware of those that are great with words - the people that know how to maneuver their words to get us to do what they want. You should also beware of people who know how to tailor their words to scar you; their words are venom. They prey on free minded people, people who are willing to take a risk and they also prey on people who don't know the truth. These people are snakes that have the ill intent to set you up for failure.

Proverbs 6:16-19 (NIV) says, *"There are six things the LORD hates, seven that are detestable to him: haughty eyes, a lying tongue, hands that shed innocent blood, a heart that devises wicked schemes, feet that are quick to rush into evil, a false witness who pours out lies and a person who stirs up conflict in the community."*

There are two types of serpents that you must be aware of - the venomous python and the anaconda. If you are dealing with someone that has anaconda-like character, you sometimes don't know it until you feel like you are being suffocated by them. But if you are still alive, you can still get out of the grip of the anaconda in your life. The anaconda drains the strength out of you by using pressure. This pressure will mostly be through words. You will often hear these types of people question your ability to do something through dares, challenges and through words such as *"if you are this, then prove it by doing that"* or in romantic relationships they say things like, *"if you love me then do this..."* In reality, these snakes suffocate their prey with each breath that the prey takes, and they squeeze their prey to the point of breaking its bones. After breaking the bones and suffocating the prey, the victim is then swallowed whole. Have you been the prey of a person with anaconda tactics? Has someone broken your backbone of boldness? It's time to cut the head off that snake, figuratively speaking!

For those that are pythons - they attack their prey in a different way. From what I've learned, not all pythons are venomous - but I am going to be speaking on venomous python characteristics. With these types of people, they always present an ultimatum to place you in a situation to choose them over another alternative. Venomous people use their words to their advantage, and they understand how to use their words to control you - whether they are painful words directly or indirectly. In nature, pythons attack their prey by striking, opening its mouth and latching its teeth into the prey. Then it wraps its body around the prey so its victim has nowhere to run. How many times have you found yourself as a victim to a person with a python spirit? Have you been attacked, stricken by their fangs? Have you experienced the venom from their words and the squeeze of the pressure from their manipulative ways? We have all been snake bitten before. Who has bitten you?

At the end of it all, these types of people don't truly love you or have your best interest at heart – they just want to be in control. They are just that - serpents, whose lies have poisoned your life and your perspective on life? But now we must take a look at the true enemy at hand.

"Now the serpent was more crafty than any of the wild animals the LORD God had made. He said to the woman, "Did God really say, 'You must not eat from any tree in the garden'?" Genesis 3:1 (NIV)

The Qualified Life

The serpent was described as more crafty than any of the wild animals the LORD God had made. The definition of crafty, according to Merriam-Webster's online dictionary is, "clever at attaining one's ends by indirect and often deceptive means". This is the exact tactic that the serpent used to deceive Eve, an indirect, clever question that made her doubt what God originally told her husband. Since, we didn't go over the full detail of what God told Adam in the beginning – let's rewind a bit so you can get the full effect.

"So God created mankind in his own image, in the image of God he created them; male and female he created them. God blessed them and said to them, "Be fruitful and increase in number; fill the earth and subdue it. Rule over the fish in the sea and the birds in the sky and over every living creature that moves on the ground."

Genesis 1:27-28 (NIV)

"The Lord God took the man and put him in the Garden of Eden to work it and take care of it. And the Lord God commanded the man, 'You are free to eat from any tree in the garden; but you must not eat from the tree of the knowledge of good and evil, for when you eat from it you will certainly die'." Genesis 2:15-17 (NIV)

So, let's take all of this and put it all together...

1. God made mankind in His own image.

2. God created man.

3. God gave mankind the assignment of being fruitful AND increase in number.

4. God gave mankind the assignment to fill the earth AND subdue it.

5. God made mankind to rule on earth.

God did not make man to rule over man - unless we are talking about government and policies of that nature. But even then, when God put the first king on earth, it wasn't even His perfect will -

mankind wanted a king! That's a different topic for another book…but we have to understand that we were not made to be ruled by man - we were intended to be led and instructed by God as we ruled over the THINGS of this earth. We were all originally created to be leaders, but the truth of the matter is that not everyone will walk into leadership, however God will send His children to be positioned as leaders to make way for His glory and to make Himself known.

It is imperative that you protect yourself from serpents and any ideologies that are presented to you that are opposite of God's instruction. Many people abandon their purpose in the earth because a serpent got into their ear gates - let this not become your story. In order to combat the lies of your enemies, you must know the truth about yourself. You must understand your value and what you have to offer the world. Revelation of truth defeats every serpent.

Notes

The Qualified Life

Chapter 5: Be You

One of the biggest lies that I've been told in my life was that I wasn't good enough. Since my childhood, I've experienced various levels and scenarios of rejection that disqualified me from being accepted and loved by the people I desired love from. It all began in Kindergarten when I was told to get on my knees and be something that I did not want to be. Brace yourself...this is going to be an interesting story.

There was a girl in grade school that I wanted to be the best of friends with. She was very popular and a leader – in Kindergarten! This girl had beautiful hair, skin, had the influence of a Presidential leader, and we all wanted to be her friend. As for me, I thought I was cool – but not as cool as her. At playtime, she would gather her friends, and they would go in their clique and play house. I REALLY wanted to play with them, so I finally got the nerve to go and ask if I could play with them.

The Qualified Life

They all looked at me, then looked at her, and she approved the request. She started giving out roles on who would play what. Some got to be her sister, one got to the mother, another got to be her best friend, and I was to the side. She told me to get on my knees and be the pet. I told her I wanted to be the best friend or someone else, and she told me no, I had to be the dog or cat. And I did it – just to be accepted. This moment defined the next fifteen plus years of my life.

For years, I have unknowingly lived a life where I felt like I never fit in. I've always tried to live beyond people's beliefs about me, although many times I even doubted my ability to achieve that. As a child, I would have never thought that being told orders to get on my knees and be the house pet, would position me in a place of being the pet to people in order to receive their approval. Who would have thought that could lead to that path? After feeling like I wouldn't get peoples' approval, I was dedicated to live a life that would prove people wrong.

What I had to come to terms with while writing this book, was that no human would ever be able to fully comprehend the capacity of who God created me to be. People may have opinions about me; some may see something great within me, and some prophets may have an accurate word of what God was doing in my life – however, no man on Earth will fully unfold the totality of who God created me to be. (1 Corinthians 13:9)

You were qualified to be you before people ever had an opinion of what they think you should be.

One of the first things that you must rid yourself from is giving people power over your destiny – you were made by God.

"I tell you, my friends, do not be afraid of those who kill the body and after that can do no more. But I will show you whom you should fear:

Fear him who, after your body has been killed, has authority to throw you into hell. Yes, I tell you, fear him." Luke 12:4-5 (NIV)

You do not have to prove to people that you are bigger than what they think you are. Why? Because you belong to God and that will be put on display when He allows the time to come.

"Now to Him who is able to do exceedingly abundantly above all that we ask or think, according to the power that works in us," Ephesians 3:20 (NKJV)

Entrusted With Destiny

This situation reminds me of Joseph, in the Bible. Joseph's story is one of those jacked up stories that end up pretty good in the end…well sort of. We'll dive right into his background. Joseph was born under some bad circumstances. He was born of Rachel[2] many

2 One of two Jacob's wives

years later while Jacob was in his old age (Jacob was Joseph's father). Rachel was loved by Jacob, but was barren for years. Leah, the other wife, was hated by Jacob. Yet God opened the womb of Leah so she was able to give Jacob children, while Rachel couldn't. So, when Joseph was born, he became Jacob's favorite son.

Some of you may know the story of and how his father gave him a coat with many colors. Well, did you know that the coat was a symbol that he would receive the best part of the brother's inheritance. He was separated as the favorite of Jacob. Joseph was hated by his brothers, so much so that they had the thought of killing him. Why? Jacob was in tune with the favor of God and he was also a dreamer - a visionary.

He had dreams that he would rule over his older brothers one day and that he would be king. Arrogant? Yes. He knew that his brothers didn't like him. They didn't even call him their brother,

The Qualified Life

they called him, "son of Jacob". But Joseph felt like he had to prove something to his brothers. God revealed his destiny to him however, he took it to the head and wanted to prove that although his brothers felt some way about him – he was going to rule over them one day and had to show them that he really was someone to be liked. And it was in that spirit of arrogance, he opened the doorway to sabotage.

His brothers beat him and sold him into slavery when he was only 17 years old. In this time frame, Joseph spent some years in prison until he was summoned to interpret a dream for the officer of Egypt. Not to mention, after he got out of prison, the officer's wife falsely accused him of trying to rape her...which led to more time in prison. Fast-forward, Joseph didn't become an overseer to Pharaoh until he was 30!

He went through a lot of circumstances and rejection. But, I often wondered...what if Joseph didn't try to prove himself to his family all those times he got dreams? I've been in Joseph's shoes before. People have doubted me and hated me for the calling on my life. And I was the type to try to prove that I was "Somebody" although I was rejected by them. But, when we try to prove ourselves to people that we are "somebody", it opens the door to the enemy and gives him the opportunity to sabotage our way. And if something can be prevented, why put ourselves in situations that can cause harm to us? God gives us promises and secrets – but it doesn't mean to always broadcast them.

God can and reveal pieces of your destiny to you. It is up to you to steward your revelations well.

When I think of the process of a seed I'm reminded about how the seed is not placed on top of the ground, it is placed deep into the soil. While placed in the soil, it is protected from the elements, predators and the footsteps of people that move around on a day-today basis. And as the seed goes through the process of growth, it is all happening underground - not in plain sight for everyone to see. By the time that we see the plant, it has already gone through the rooting process deep in the soil. I believe that God uses plants to teach us a thing or two about destiny.

When we are constantly broadcasting the plans that God wants us to keep in secret, we put our seeds out to be trampled on. We can try to say, "nothing can stop the plan of God", which is true, unless you stop the plans by being disobedient to His instructions. Disobedience can bring delay to divine moments in time. You may be in a season to reap, but you can self sabotage your blessing and reap it in another season because you were not well-prepared nor properly positioned. God is sovereign, but He wants to entrust us with the precious secrets He has in store for us.

"It is He who reveals the profound and hidden things..."

Daniel 2:22 (AMP)

If God can entrust Joseph with revelation of his destiny, He can do the same for you. Something that I love about God is that He makes His plans for our lives known, so we can come into alignment with them. How can you ever walk into something that you are completely unaware of? I believe that we disqualify ourselves from knowing our future, because we think that God won't show us or speak it out to us. But His word is true when it says, *"You will show me the path of life;..."* (Psalm 16:11) oh, and another truth that His word says is, *"Your word is a lamp for my feet, a light on my path."* Psalm 119:105 (NIV) These scriptures let you know that God will speak to you and lead you regarding your future!

How amazing is that?! You don't have to live in the dark, or live by luck, He will make your future known to you! Guess what, you are qualified to be you - just align yourself with His voice and He will guide you into the right path for YOUR success. Do not waste time comparing yourself to others. Knowing the voice of God will position you in the right place at the right time. Continue to be you, (the you He wants you to be) and He will place you where you are purposed to be. The TRUTH will position you in destiny.

"This is good, and pleases God our Savior, who wants all people to be saved and to come to a knowledge of the truth."

1 Timothy 2:3-4 (NIV)

Notes

The Qualified Life

Chapter 6: Live

There have been multiple times when people have come across my life, that feel like they don't have a reason to live. Honestly, in the past I had moments where I was in a place of vulnerability, I would hear whispers within me that would say things like, "you should just kill yourself...no one cares about you. If you just kill yourself you don't have to deal with this anymore. It's not like you have anything else to do in this life...you can just kill yourself". I just felt alone, like a failure, because life didn't seem to be changing anytime soon.

It is in the moments of idle thinking, deep sorrow, rejection and/or trauma where demonic spirits find the opportunity to plant the seeds of suicide in the mind. Sometimes these thoughts that replay in your mind can sometimes be words that people have said to you that create thoughts of rejection.

The Qualified Life

"For we wrestle not against flesh and blood, but against principalities, against powers, against the rulers of the darkness of this world, against spiritual wickedness in high places." Ephesians 6:12 (KJV)

This is a constant battle that we are engaged in – and it is spiritual. These thoughts of suicide that come into the mind is not originated from you – it is from spiritual, wicked beings in the spirit realm. This is bigger than the physical life that you see. These enemies have strategies, they have powers, these are rulers and they are wicked. I am going to break this down some more for you:

The greek word for powers in Ephesians 6:12 is translated to the word *Exousia (Strongs #1832)* which translates to four meanings, but I will be focusing on two definitions and how these two definitions will give further understanding of the battle over and in your life.

Powers of Legal Rights

Exousia has a definition which focuses on *the power of rule or government (the power of him whose will and commands must be submitted to by others and obeyed).*

Jesus preached about the Kingdom of God, read about it in the Gospels. A kingdom is a form of government, so this is why we must cover the basics of the Kingdom.

"After this, Jesus traveled about from one town and village to another, proclaiming the good news of the kingdom of God. The Twelve were with him," Luke 8:1 (NIV)

There are systems and protocols in place when it comes to the Kingdom of God. If you are from America, this could be somewhat of a challenge to understand.

The way that the spirit realm works is by way of authority but it goes by the systems of a kingdom. When I first heard about the Kingdom of God it was a challenge to process – being that in America we have a president and not a king. We live in a democracy, where our nation's citizens can participate in the making of laws, policies, impeachment and even our structure as a nation. However, with a kingdom – that isn't so.

A kingdom has a king, citizens, laws, rights, inheritances, military units and territory. The king of a kingdom is responsible for his kingdom's protection, resources, rights and the expansion of his rule. A president can have other sources of government above him; however, a king is the sovereign ruler over his land through inheritance or monarchy. He has final say of all laws, structures and policies. Family members of kings and queens have special privileges and are honored because their name is associated with their king. Kings have rulership that stretches for generations and the throne continues through family bloodline or war. A president's rulership isn't inherited – it is voted by the people.

Another definition for *Exousia* is, *the power of authority (influence) and of right (privilege).* When dealing with a kingdom, there are legal rights and laws that are set in place that must be obeyed. If there are laws that are in place, and those laws are not obeyed – there are consequences. Most of the time when laws are broken, citizens either experience prison or death. Citizens are protected by the law and have access to certain privileges of the nations by their rights as kingdom citizens.

This helps understand how the Kingdom of God works.

"After this, Jesus traveled about from one town and village to another, proclaiming the good news of the kingdom of God. The Twelve were with him," Luke 8:1 (NIV)

Jesus not only preached, but He demonstrated the power that He possessed. Why? Lives depended on it - they depended on Him coming into His power. Without power, the powerless would die. Jesus not only came to give life to those that physically died, but He also revived those who were spiritually dead. The enemy of your soul wants you to abandon the calling on your life - which is suicide. So how do we live? Rise to the occasion of recognizing you are called to be powerful and called to dethrone the powers of darkness in your life and the life of others.

The Agenda Of Suicide

What people must understand is the agenda and the power that is given over when someone commits suicide. When a person decides to do this, they are not only taking away a LIFE from the population of the human civilization on earth, but they also rob a piece of another individual's destiny. Your life is connected to another person's hope. Everyone was created to impact at least one person in their lifetime; just think about how many people there are in the world! As a human being, you were given the power to influence. Now, what we choose to do with that influence is up to us - whether that be good or bad influence. With that being said, if you have a gift to motivate people, and you decide not to use it, you rob people from being motivated to press on another day.

Can you imagine what life would be like if the creator of Uber decided to give up? We wouldn't have an amazing app which helps people get around! Imagine a world without the mind of Steve Jobs...or Bill Gates! The world of innovation wouldn't be what it is today. The world wouldn't be what it is today without you. Think about this: If you are considering suicide (whether that be suicide of your life's purpose or physical suicide), there is somebody out there that is in the same mindset who is waiting for someone to give them hope - just like you're hoping someone would motivate and encourage you. And if you decide to end your life - they won't have YOU to give them hope.

Now don't get me wrong, you are not their god. However, you are the person in place to be a voice of hope in a time of desperation. Sometimes we ask God to help us, and of course He is our help, but most of the time the help that He sends will be through a human being. That is why we must be willing to be real about where we currently are in our state of mind AND our current circumstances.

How many times have you told someone, *"I'm fine"* but in reality, you were struggling, busted and disgusted by the way that your current life circumstances were looking? If Jesus died on the cross for you...and rose again so you can rise...why should you check out of life because things seem hard, for now? Death cannot save you. On the other side of death, without God, is an eternity without hope - hell. (2 Thessalonians 1:7-9, ESV) So imagine, the hopelessness you are currently experiencing, multiplied and repeated for eternity.

If you have found yourself in this place in your life, I want to encourage you to set your hope upon the Lord and His word.

"I rise before dawn and cry for help; I have put my hope in your

word." Psalm 110:147 (NIV)

"Praise be to the God and Father of our Lord Jesus Christ! In his great mercy he has given us new birth into a living hope through the resurrection of Jesus Christ from the dead, and into an inheritance that can never perish, spoil or fade. This inheritance is kept in heaven for you, who through faith are shielded by God's power until the coming of the salvation that is ready to be revealed in the last time. In all this you greatly rejoice, though now for a little while you may have had to suffer grief in all kinds of trials." 1 Peter 1:3-6 (NIV)

Your life is worth living.

Back to the point of the agenda of suicide: The devil wants to make you blind to your potential, your value and your ability to extend hope - and the way that he chooses to do this with some, is through thoughts of suicide. Someone is waiting for you to come into the understanding of who you are and the revelation of God in you to be revealed in the fullness. If you do not know your value, you can't offer this to someone who is in need.

"For the creation waits in eager expectation for the children of God to be revealed." Romans 8:19 (NIV)

Spiritual Suicide

Maybe you don't deal with thoughts of suicide, but you have abandoned your faith. Have you felt stagnant in your faith? Have you lost your fire and zeal for the things of God? If so, you may be experiencing a spiritual death. Some have committed "spiritual suicide" by choosing not to grow spiritually. This can happen by not reading the word of God, not listening to the words of God and ultimately, not having a current relationship with Him.

There was a time that I didn't know that I was spiritually numb and unmotivated. I felt the affects of it but I didn't know that it was my spiritual state. Unfortunately, we can depend on our old encounters with God as though they are our present reality...and then have the audacity to make them the reflection of our current standing with God. This is not a safe mentality to have, it's dangerous. Think of it as using dial up internet speed from the early 2000's in modern day time - it's not up to date so it will malfunction. We must have a current, daily relationship with God. Can you imagine getting married to someone, but never have any type of intimacy or communication? Imagine, standing on the fact that you talked a lot during the dating phase, and assuming your marriage must be currently good because it was good back then. That relationship is dead! You must have fresh intimacy, daily communication and a commitment that is evident in the way that you live.

This same principle applies to our relationship with God! You cannot act as though your past experiences with Him are relevant now, He wants something new, and fresh - today.

The Qualified Life

"I am crucified with Christ: nevertheless I live; yet not I, but Christ liveth in me: and the life which I now live in the flesh I live by the faith of the Son of God, who loved me, and gave himself for me."

Galatians 2:20 (KJV)

"You were taught, with regard to your former way of life, to put off your old self, which is being corrupted by its deceitful desires; to be made new in the attitude of your minds; and to put on the new self, created to be like God in true righteousness and holiness."

Ephesians 4:22-24 (NIV)

"I will give them an undivided heart and put a new spirit in them; I will remove from them their heart of stone and give them a heart of flesh."

Ezekiel 11:9 (NIV)

If you desire to resurrect your spiritual life, there are a few things to get in order:

1.   Accept that you're imperfect and God still loves you despite your imperfection.

Does this mean to continue in sin because you're not perfect? No! It means that although you may fall, God's mercy is still there to redeem you. No matter where you are in life, God wants to meet you there and give you a new beginning.

2.   You must let your old life go and take hold of your new life which is Christ living through you.

Have you made idols and trophies from old achievements? Eliminate the pride that keeps you stuck in your past achievements so God can do something new. Your past is the past, it is not the present. *Without faith, it is impossible to please God.* So, is your faith currently active or is it from some time ago? *God rewards those who diligently seek Him,* so if you aren't doing this currently, what is your reward? (Hebrews 11:6 NIV)

It's time to live a life in a new direction with a fresh start - as though your past has no negative influence on your future..

3.   Receive the Holy Spirit

"He said unto them, Have ye received the Holy Ghost since ye believed?

And they said unto him, ``We have not so much as heard

whether there be any Holy Ghost." Acts 19:2

Have you received the Holy Spirit since you believed in Jesus? I ain't talking about dancing and shouting - I'm talking about a transformed, power filled life! The Bible tells us that when you are baptized with the Holy Ghost, you receive power!

"But ye shall receive power, after that the Holy Ghost is come upon

you: and ye shall be witnesses unto me both in Jerusalem, and in all Judaea, and in Samaria, and unto the uttermost part of

the earth." Acts 1:8

The power of the Holy Ghost will give you power to walk in miracles and give you access to Heaven's doings. When you have been FILLED with the Holy Ghost, not only will you be transformed, others around you will be impacted. This is what Stephen the Evangelist experienced in Acts 6:8, *"And Stephen, full of faith and power, did great wonders and miracles among the people." (KJV)*

The Holy Ghost gives you power and makes you a witness of God's goodness and His current works! You are meant to live a life filled with the Holy Ghost, anything apart from that is power-less.

"Do you not know that your bodies are temples of the Holy Spirit, who is in you, whom you have received from God? You are not your own;"

1 Corinthians 6:19 (NIV)

The Holy Ghost will fill you, help you, give you hope and a new life!

The Qualified Life

I have to give you some Greek root words when it comes to the Holy Ghost so you can see the importance of Him...I'm so stirred up as I'm writing this! The Bible calls the Holy Ghost the Comforter; the transliteration according to Strong's G3875 for Comforter is *paraklētos* which means *an intercessor, consoler:—advocate, comforter. Properly, summoned, called to one's side, especially called to one's aid; hence, "one who pleads another's cause before a judge, a pleader, counsel for defense, legal assistant; an advocate"*

This right here will set you free! YOU ARE NOT ALONE WHEN YOU RECEIVE THE HOLY GHOST! You have someone that pleads on your behalf; you have a counselor and someone who is there to be your aid - the Holy Ghost! This is why it is imperative that as a Believer in Christ, that you receive your Helper! You can't do this by yourself, you were meant to receive help/an aide/ a comforter, after you believe in Jesus.

This is why people leave the faith - they haven't **received** since they believed! You are endowed with power when you receive the Holy Spirit of God. Receive Him just as they did in Acts 2. Find a true person that is filled with the power of the Holy Ghost to pray with you to receive Him; and as you receive Him, you will receive new tongues and a new, power filled life!

4. Go through the process of God to mold **and** soften your heart.

When we allow God to soften our heart, our heart becomes receptive to His word which allows us to be formed into who He wants us to be. You can't shape hard clay, but you can make a masterpiece when it's soft. The same thing applies to our heart, God can mold a soft heart. Your relationship with God and your faith in His word is what helps you overcome the devil. There is no way that you have a relationship with God by **only** reading the word; because God is alive, He speaks. Your relationship with Him requires communication and obedience to His word.

The Qualified Life

You are qualified to live naturally and spiritually. If you desire to live a fulfilled life, it starts from the inside - your spirit. Your spirit must be aligned with God on a day to day basis - there is spiritual maintenance that you must keep up with. This is a requirement of a consistent prayer life, positioning yourself to hear Him, a consistent lifestyle of reading His word AND living His word out. If we can get our spirit renewed, we can truly enjoy our lives as we remain in Him. You are never alone when you receive Him. It's time to live - spiritually and naturally, with your hope and future anchored in the Lord. Be fulfilled by being filled with the Holy Ghost and your life will never be the same!

Notes

The Qualified Life

Chapter 7: Influence

Everyone was born with the *potential* to be a leader. It's in our DNA; we were crafted to be leaders. But you must understand that leadership is firstborn out of the heart of servant-hood. No leader can lead effectively without having a heart to serve people. You must know what is like to serve people before you try to lead them into a destination.

True influencers can be entrusted to those who can be trusted with a promised destination of "the next level" - I call them "Level Up Leaders". Being a level up leader is choosing to live a lifestyle of example. Of course, not everyone will be a CEO of a company, but you are definitely qualified to live a life of being an example to others. How do you treat people, daily? Can people depend on you to be a helping hand? Truthfully evaluate your heart of servant-hood before trying to set up a platform for yourself.

Advancement

When you are positioned on a job, you learn skills for a reason. You weren't made to stay at an entry level worker for the rest of your life - you are supposed to advance. Why? So you can raise up the next generation of people that come into the company. Do you understand how degrading it is to live a lower level position for the rest of your life without the fulfillment of advancement? You'll begin to hate your job. If you desire to only stay at stage 1, you have to change your perspective, gain vision and motivation from someone that can lead you onto a path of success. What would keep you from advancing in your life?

If you've been entrusted with a job, you've been entrusted with the potential to advance. The company saw potential in you and wanted you to help their company advance into the future. Some jobs, they are complete scams, yes - but you have the potential inside you to be a leader for those that are coming up after you.

You were created with a gift/ability to impact this world. A gift must be identified, cultivated and placed on display for people to see. But if no one ever told you this, you have most likely found yourself in a stagnant, dissatisfied place in life. I've met many people in my short lifetime that are convinced that they have nothing to offer the world. I always hear people say, "I'm not talented". When I hear this from complete strangers, my first question is, why? What makes you think that you are not talented? And if they don't have a talent, my next thing is to ask, what are you gifted in?

Did you know that what you consider talented/gifted is only 20% of what a gift is considered? There are various gifts and those gifts were created to be made for influence. In the following paragraphs, you will discover the different realms of influence, what gifts are and how you can use them for your advancement.

Gifts vs. Talent

Everyone is born with a gift, but not everyone was born talented. A gift is something that was instilled in you and blossomed from you since your entrance into this world. Have you ever seen a child gravitate towards drawing and as they grew, their gift improved, naturally? Or maybe you've noticed how someone was naturally given a gift to motivate people, or naturally born with a fashion sense - "it was just them". This is the sign of a gift - it was in them from the very beginning and it is just their nature to do it.

A talent is different, because a talent can be learned. There are many people who can learn something, but that doesn't mean that they were destined to do it. There are many talents that I have learned, but that doesn't qualify me as someone to advance others in it. Everything in our life should be purposeful and intentional. Everything that we do should advance and enhance us. If we are simply doing things without a reason, we waste time. Myles Munroe said it best, "time is the currency of life"; and if we waste time, we waste our life. Our gifts are meant to be a blessing to others - it should not be handled selfishly. If I have something that has the ability to help people and change the world, how does it help me if I withhold it from people?

Now that I've established those facts, I want to establish that there are different types of gifts - natural and spiritual.

"There are different gifts, but the same Spirit. There are different ministries, but the same Lord. There are different ways of working, but the same God works all things in all men." 1 Corinthians 12:4-6

There are spiritual gifts that God has given and these gifts are to be understood as GIFTS. A gift is offered and it is a choice to receive the gift or not. We must combine our natural gifts with our spiritual gifts to bring heaven on earth in our realm of influence. Let's discuss where your gift can be used in places of influence:

Government

Were you the type of kid that wanted to be a lawyer, police officer or even the President during play time? This may have been a destiny moment for you. Where in the world would the earth be if there weren't people in place to direct justice and order? It's great to have a government, however we are all aware that there are corrupt officials in the high chairs of government offices. There are governors, senators and officials that create policies, taxes, laws and delayed responses to injustice in order to oppress the poor and minorities. They also put these policies and taxes in place to grow their own pockets.

We need a positive change in the government - people that are going to act with integrity and are willing to create beneficial policies for the people that live normal lives from day to day. Every state needs representatives and governors in place to look to make sure that there is equality. The world needs police officers that will be fair when it comes to protecting and serving our communities. No one should fear the police when they see them drive by, that is unnatural. We need protection over fear.

Corrupt police officers must be exposed. There should be no reason that there are police officers working with drug dealers for money. Racist police officials must be exposed! There should be no way in the world that police officers can have a membership in racist confederate hate groups and hold a police badge. Getting paid to execute blacks and minorities is injustice - and it needs to be exposed and dealt with.

We can't sit on the sidelines when we know that something is stirring on the inside of us to make and be the difference. Do you see how important these jobs are? Maybe that person is you. Will you take your place to bring change and speak out on injustice in that system

The Qualified Life

Media / Entertainment / Arts

Calling all actors, singers, producers, painters and entertainers...there is a casting call with your name on it. The headline reads, "Take Your Place!" You are in the line up to make a difference in the world by using your gifts. Are you a writer, a visionary that can bring art to life? The world is waiting for your creativity to come forth. To me, it's obvious how your gift can influence lives, but I am going to give you some understanding if you don't see why YOU can make the difference.

If you are an artist using pencils, pens, graphic designing and colors, the world is influenced by your imagination on paper. We need you to draw blueprints for buildings, for creating visual artistry to be stored as memories in museums. Art speaks volumes and can show emotions and bring healing to the soul. A reason that many people go to the museum is to experience peace or awe when they look at the work. Your art is meant to impact lives, it is meant to build enterprises, stadiums, sanctuaries and more. Artists are the foundation for building the future. There are people waiting on your creativity and innovation to make the world, the future.

Artists build the future. Without visual art, the world lacks vision; and where there is no vision there is nothing and no one to build the future.

Are you a poet, expressive with words creating stories to bring imaginations into wonder? Write, now! The world needs your words to create new wonder. Without your expression, how will we ever know the creative mind and words that God wants to release onto the earth? Your words matter, and they have the power to shape the future and history!

Education

The world is in need of educators to teach upcoming generations the fundamentals of life AND how to make the future, bigger and better.

The Qualified Life

Without education there is nothing to build. Educators have the capacity and ability to change the course of destinies. Have you ever had an amazing teacher that had an impact on your life...to the point where you still remember the name of that teacher today? Yeah, that's the power of an educator with the ability to impact someone's future.

Educators help students understand complicated concepts and new ideas in a way that is easy to comprehend and digest. We need educators because knowledge is meant to be passed down. Impactful educators make education fun, and they also understand how to make sure that each student is taught in their own unique way. Generation changing educators pass on wisdom - making sure that they can speak into the future of individuals.

Sound wisdom has the ability to change the course of someone's future.

I remember an English teacher I had in high school who spoke into my future. At that time, I had just got out of a relationship and immediately went into another one. My teacher pulled me aside and said, *"Veonne, you are too beautiful to be going from one relationship to another. You are worth more than that."* Mr. Brown really impacted me that day - he had me questioning my whole life. I also recall in middle school where there was a math teacher that totally changed my potential when it came to math. I ABSOLUTELY HATED MATH...I still don't like it, but my 8th grade teacher made it easier for me to understand. Out of my entire middle school career, my 8th grade year was the only year that I didn't have to spend my summer vacation in summer school, why? That teacher made math less complicated, and I passed the course. In my short time as a teacher, I talked two students that had suicidal thoughts and they said that I changed their lives after talking with them. Educators change destinies - and they can save lives!

The Qualified Life

Teachers/Educators are there to challenge your limits on what you think you are capable of achieving; they bring out the best in you. The greatest teachers I've experienced challenged me to get out of my comfort zones. Educators identify your strengths and challenge your comfort zones (stagnancy) and uses strengths to overpower the weaknesses. They don't keep you in a place of weakness and discouragement, they feed you with knowledge and understanding making you strong and overcome your weaknesses.

Science / Health Industry

There is nothing more appreciative in life than when a life is brought into the world and when a life is saved from death. I recall the appreciation I had when me and my daughter were on the brink of dying during her birth. I viewed life as a precious opportunity after this experience. If it were not for those doctors in the hospital, we wouldn't be here today. We need doctors and scientists to advance in our health and scientific industries. Think about the importance of having scientists that create medicines and cures for diseases, not to mention common illnesses that people experience on a day-to-day basis. The world needs doctors, scientists and nurses; without them, we lack solutions and innovation.

Never should you allow stereotypes to keep you from becoming a scientist or doctor - you can be who you decide to be. There are people whose life depends on your step of faith to be that nutritionist, nurse, dentist, scientific innovator or surgeon that you may be considering to be. Invest in your future, go to college, study to show yourself worthy of the cause - you were made to be a game changer. Maybe you are the one to create that incurable disease. The best way to get the cure is to be connected to the Creator of all good things. God's word tells us that the Holy Spirit will lead us and guide us into ALL truth - that includes cures, insight and wisdom in the fields of science and health. God is a Healer, but He can also heal through you. Are you the one to make a difference in this industry?

The Qualified Life

Business/Finance

Many people are called to the realm of finance and business. These individuals provide solutions to problems and gain capital (money) to solve that problem (that's all a business really is). If someone doesn't feel like cooking, they pay someone to cook for them. If a business needs a service to add value, they hire a contractor. This realm is a problem solving realm with the ability to bless people from their solution AND the ability to bless people with their gains. Maybe you're a philanthropist, what problem will you solve with your influence?

Religion

There is such a responsibility when it comes to being entrusted as one to be a leader in the faith. Sacrifice, submission, servant hood and sanctification are the foundations of a daily lifestyle when being an influence in this realm. I have found that there are many people that become pastors, but have not been called by God to do so. When it comes to becoming a religious influence, I advise wise, Godly, seasoned counsel. I also advise that you become a master learner and do-er of God's word.

Religion is the most powerful influence upon the earth - and even political leaders know this. THAT is why it is very critical that people are aware that not everyone is called to this responsibility. Not everyone is called to start a church, not everyone is called to pastor - and that is completely fine. We do more damage when we do things that we are not called to do.

It is wonderful to be a solution as a leader of the faith! There are many people that look to religion as a means of hope - or the only hope that they have. This type of leadership affects communities, cultures and daily living. Being this type of leader allows you to be used by God to raise up people, change the community through the transforming power of God, provide a place where miracles can happen and most importantly, display the love and power of God wherever you are.

Conclusion

Influence is something that many want to have, but are not willing to be processed for. There is so much responsibility that comes with influence, not only because everyone is watching - but ultimately because God is watching. The way that we live our lives will be accounted for.

"So then every one of us shall give account of himself to God." Romans 14:12 (KJV)

We've gone over the difference between gifts and talent, to find that you have a gift! Your mission is to now discover what that gift is and where will you use your gift to be that influence?

You are qualified to influence!

Notes

The Qualified Life

Chapter 8: Keys For Success

Have you ever been afraid of the thought of being successful? I have! The fear of success is rooted in the fear of the unknown. For years, I battled with this because I feared that I would not know what to do when I got to a place of success…would I even be able to identify it if I were in it? I feared becoming prideful, a lover of money and forgetting those who loved me in my lowest moments. **If you fear that you won't know what to do when you get to the place of success or an anticipated destination for your future, you will never get there.** Why? When you fear the unknown, you'll always play it safe. And playing it safe will make you repeat patterns to never walk in a realm of creating new experiences. Fear of the unknown creates destructive habits and cycles.

The Qualified Life

When you fear the unknown, you will form the following habits:

1.   Making excuses on why you shouldn't pursue it.

This includes but not limited to saying you're waiting on God's perfect timing.

2.   Losing focus when it comes to finishing projects/assignments.

3.   Not accepting help or advice from people who can bring you help.

4.   Having pity parties.

5.   Talking about it but not being about it.

However, in this chapter I am going to be teaching you why you qualify for success, how to overcome the fear of success and 6 keys that are required to walk into the best, successful life.

Success In Your DNA

There was a time in my life where I experienced the fear of success...however my fear of success was a unique situation. Usually when people fear success, they fear the unknown, but my fear was tied into that…but the source of it all was fear of my true potential. There was a war on the inside of me - a war of not being the very best that I could be. One of the reasons I knew this was because I would find myself in situations where I knew what I had to do to get somewhere, however I wouldn't go with it all the way through. It took years for me to really take the time to understand that EVERYONE has the capability of being successful - it's in our DNA. But what we must understand is what we are made of and made for.

In order to really understand that you were made for success, you need to know what you were made to be successful for and in. We were all designed with abilities and qualities that make us unique - well crafted creations. Just think about how each and every human being on earth has a special fingerprint, we are all different. And with these special features, abilities and qualities in our character - we have the capability to change the worlds of people, cultures, times and places of influences. However, when you do not know what makes YOU (twofold) and how you are able to change worlds,

The Qualified Life

cultures, times and places of influence - you will live in an unqualified world.

Made By & Made For

It is easy to find success in the things that make us the most money. Trust me, I've been there. I couldn't count how many start-ups I've been involved in to see crash and burn. What you must understand is that success is not equivalent to just money. You can have the most "success" with billions of dollars and still be out of touch with what you were designed to do in this life.

The world is full of people who are busy without finding true fulfillment and social change for the greater good of the earth. You don't change the world by being busy, you change it by doing what you were created to do.

How many millionaires and celebrities have we seen in the world that has found themselves in addictions, destructive

129

relationships and/or have committed suicide? Too many to count. This lets us know that success isn't in gaining a platform to display your money, talents and abilities for the world to see.

Success is in the ability to create solutions for the problems within the world, using Divine strategies, reform and social change from Heaven to earth - through the gift that is hidden within you.

You're now probably wondering - how do I do that? Well first, you must know Who created you.

"For You created my inmost being; You knit me together in my mother's womb." Psalm 139:13 (NIV)

Who is the, *You* in this segment?

"The LORD reclaimed you. He formed you in the womb. This is what the LORD says: I, the LORD, made everything. I stretched out the heavens by myself. I spread out the earth all alone." Isaiah 44:24 (GW)

The Qualified Life

Ah, yes - the Lord. It is impossible to know your true potential and level of greatness without knowing your Creator.

Key #1 - Know Your Steps

One of the greatest leaders that had lived on earth, Dr. Myles Munroe made mention that as creations, we must know how the Creator made us to function by knowing what's in the instruction manual - His Word. Now, His Word is twofold. There is the *logos* which is the written word, and there is the *rhema* word which is His now word - by revelation. The Lord can give *rhema* word through using His voice to you personally - which He prefers the most, a person who has been sent to tell you the word of the Lord, He can use signs and words as well - He's not limited in how He communicates to you. God's *rhema* word will never contradict His *logos* word - which is the scriptures. But you must have both His now word with the scripture combined to live an effective life.

How do you get to know the voice of the Lord to gain direction for your life? It begins with "that gut feeling" that you get sometimes. Have you ever been in a situation where "you felt something" was telling you not to do something because so-and-so would happen? Yep, that was most likely God. But when it comes to hearing God for instruction for your life, it requires a relationship with Him. He's not that person that you just get to know in order to get things done - He has feelings and concerns for your well-being. What type of relationship is required? *"For as many as are led by the Spirit of God, these are sons of God."* which is mentioned in Romans 8:14.

The key to hearing the voice of God is to be a child of God; and the way to be a child of God is to have faith in Christ Jesus.

Galatians 3:26 (NLT) says it plainly "For you are all children of God through faith in Christ Jesus." And how do you get to know Christ? By studying, obeying and knowing His word because He is His word (John 1:1). How can you be led by something that you do not know? That's like riding in a car with a complete stranger - you'd probably have issues trusting the person driving the car listening to them tell you that they are going to take you somewhere special, right? God wants you to get to know Him and His truth. Sure, He'll reveal some great things about where He's taking you in life - but ultimately, He wants you to know who He is and His perfect will for each day. And having your steps ordered by God daily is the first step to success. What you'll find is as you know Him, you'll discover His will reflects His standard for your life.

Step #2 - Know Your Place

The second key to success is to truthfully identify where you currently are in life. Are you currently struggling? If so, who have you reached out to for help? Many...actually all of my biggest failures occurred because I overestimated myself, looked to my own ability and refused to communicate what my life was currently experiencing at that moment in time. I remember when I was homeless - many people didn't know that I was…suffering in silence. If I had opened my mouth instead of letting my pride get the best of me, I would have had a place to live. Who said I had to live in a car? Who said that I HAD TO struggle?

Some of your life experiences don't have to be a process, they just need to be communicated to be fixed.

It's a shame that we accept poverty as "our process" when God never said that we had to live in poverty. When the Bible tells us that we will experience suffering - that does not mean and/or include lack. If God is the supplier of our needs, and He lets us know that we are supposed to be living an abundant life, why do we say that staying in poverty is a part of our process? Poverty is the complete opposite of what Jesus did for us on the cross. If He died, so we don't have to lack, why would He make that a part of our process? It's contradicting what He did for us on the cross!

The Qualified Life

Don't allow your pride to keep you from communicating that you need help. Success is attained when you have partnerships. It's easy to try to do it yourself…but in reality, it ends up being harder. Without people, you can achieve nothing. You need people for resources. Consumers are people. PEOPLE ARE A NECESSITY FOR SUCCESS - you can't do it without them. And if you are currently in a place in your life where you have a vision to get something done you won't have the proper resources to attain success without developing a network of people.

Robert J. Watkins did a teaching on YouTube called, *How To Build Wealth & A Team At The Same Time* where he highlighted the types of people that you need to create a successful team: a visionary/innovator, a mechanic (strong at creating systems), a public relations communicator, supporters (investors) behind the scenes, a deal maker concerned with dealing with money and a landlord able to thrive outside economic crisis. As you can see, you can't be successful by yourself because you will kill yourself trying to fulfill all of these roles on your own. I've tried it and burned out. **You may be multifaceted but you are not called to do everything yourself.** This is why God created other people, because we succeed - together.

Usually, people who try to do everything on their own feel like they have to prove something to people who doubted them. You don't have to prove anything to anyone. I really don't believe in those quotes where they say success is the best revenge. Why? What is the point of living successful to prove the haters wrong? Just be. It's time for us to just be great, without feeling the obligation to prove them wrong. The best success is being the greatest version of yourself without the thought of what other people think of you. It's draining to constantly live a life to prove people wrong. I'd rather just do it and if they feel a certain way, then so be it. But I refuse to allow my success to be revenge to people who doubted me. That feeling will never be enough, because you will constantly try to 1 up your last "success". Evaluate where you are and who you need to be to get where you are going. From the list of people that are needed to have a successful team and build wealth, which person do you most identify with? And also, who are the people you need on your team to walk into your purpose?

Key #3 - Know Your Stuff Enough To Be An Expert

I've always been a multifaceted person when it comes to displaying talents, however I wasn't an expert in every field. Some of my talents include graphic designing, drawing, web design and acting. With all these different talents, I had to identify what were the areas that I wanted to make into a skill. America has many people in the world that want to do everything, but are experts in nothing. When you are not an expert, you leave room for mediocrity.

When I worked in corporate America, I had many talents, but in my career they asked what my skills were. Stumped, I put graphic designing - since I did that for some years. But little did I know, when being a freelancer I developed the skill of sales. So in my career as a sales rep, I groomed my gift in being a saleswoman to apply that skill in my own business. All the personality and zeal that I had come together in the realm of sales. I was then awarded for having the best attitude in my entire business development department in our region. The irony in this is that I was going through the hardest time of my life when I was awarded with this. It was during the time my marriage was on the rocks and I would literally cry at work because I was overwhelmed by what I was mentally going through. The CEO of the company didn't know what I was going through, neither did the managers - but they saw the smile I would have every day when I would come in. Although I would cry at my desk, at lunch and in the bathroom, I was determined to make sure someone else smiled. My goal was to always make someone smile, no matter what I was going through.

With all of that being said - what is a skill that you have to offer the world? Your skills will open the door to big opportunities. Wherever you go, there is a problem that needs to be solved - but in order for it to be solved there needs to be a skill in place. **You need to know your stuff - educate yourself in your skill.** If you need to become certified - become certified. If you need a degree or more, get your degree! Your success has requirements and you must get equipped with what you need to thrive.

We are living in a time when you have to be able to create your own success, be great by accepting yourself and doing whatever it takes to get where you need to go. One of the greatest things that I could have done in my life was educating myself in my skill-set. If you don't know what you are talking about, the systems of your industry or you don't advance your knowledge in your skill - you will become irrelevant. You've got to know your stuff - educate yourself in your skill and become an expert.

You are responsible for your success.

What are you passionate about that can become a skill that you can be expert in?

It's also wisdom to get a mentor in your skill-set. You need to be able to have someone guide you where you've never been. A mentor places you onto a path of success because they know the steps to take in order for you to become who you've never been.

Key #4 - Know Your Tribe

Whatever your skill is, there are a particular group of people that need what you have to offer - it's called your target audience. In marketing, you can also call your target audience your niche/tribe. When I think of a tribe, I think of a cultural type of people who believe, think and do things a particular way. Who is your tribe? Let me break it down into another way of saying this: who are the people you are called to? Who are the people that you are called to make a difference in?

What is the message of revelation and revolution that you are going to communicate to your tribe? When you can discover this, the last step to take is to know the solution for your tribe's need. A tribe has a language in which they relay information and a language in which they receive information. They also have a particular need that needs to be met. If you want to meet their needs, you have to be able to speak their language. Now, some of you may be thinking, "well, if I go to another country to offer food to starving people and I do not speak their language, I can still provide the solution for them".

You may have been able to provide a temporary solution, but that solution will not be a change that can impact the future generations if you cannot speak their language. If you are expecting to make significant change, that change must be envisioned to be universal and generational.

Key #5 - Know The Solution & Your Results

When you can speak a language of a people, you can then partner with them to create systems in place to provide future solutions for future possibilities. If you can find a solution for the future, you are set up to experience success.

Think of Uber. They were able to create a solution for people who don't have access to transportation - genius! They didn't even start out with inventory, but they were able to identify a need of a people. Their tribe: people who were without transportation but willing to pay for the ride across town. Uber was able to speak to their lack of transportation and frustration due to that problem. Uber also provided jobs for people who had transportation. There were many people in America with transportation but without jobs. Many of those people had dreams of living a life of entrepreneurship - and Uber provided a flexible schedule for them to work whenever they wanted to, using their transportation.

You have a people to reach and a problem to solve. In order to solve that problem, create a plan and system in order for it to continue while you are not there. When you can create a system, you can raise up future leaders to do the same.

Step #6 - Stay humble.

"Pride leads to disgrace, but with humility comes wisdom." Proverbs 11:2 (NLT) This truth makes me think of a moment in my childhood where I vividly remember a hilarious, prideful moment. It was fifth grade, and I officially made an enemy with a girl in my class. She was very loud and rude; I guess she felt like the world revolved around her. Well, one day we had a big argument in class and I made the statement, "that's why your hair is fake." She had on a fake pin on ponytail and I knew that it would get under her skin. She responded, "this is my hair! You're just mad because your hair doesn't look like this." Next thing we see, as she begins spinning her hair to taunt me, her ponytail flew across the classroom. Boy o boy, from that moment on she wasn't as vocal as she used to be. Why did I tell this story? Pride will have you in situations that gravitate humiliation and exposure. It's very sad, but true.

To be honest, I am grateful for that principle in life - it keeps people humble. Sometimes you may not find yourself in a humiliated state publically, but you may find yourself in circumstances which make you humble and relatable to those who have gone through similar circumstances. When I lost everything, it humbled me. I knew what it was like to go through loss, and I discovered how to be grateful when I did have everything. **Loss makes you realize how much you take for granted.** So, if you find yourself experiencing the loss of material things, it could have been that you prioritized material things over the things that truly matter. God is sovereign, but sometimes our actions and decisions place us in the circumstances that we experience. What I love about God's promises is that He keeps them. He is faithful even when we are not. Look at this promise for those that walk with God,

"God, your God, will restore everything you lost; he'll have compassion on you; he'll come back and pick up the pieces from all the places where you were scattered." Deuteronomy 30:3 (MSG)

He promises us that he will restore everything that you lost - because He has compassion! The pieces of your life that were broken, He will pick them up and make you whole.

"No branch can bear fruit by itself; it must remain in the vine. Neither can you bear fruit unless you remain in me." (John 15:4)

The War Over Your Success

Sometimes we think that we are being held back by "something" - and we are absolutely right. There is literally a war against your mind to keep you from being successful. You may constantly find yourself having to fight against the thoughts of doubts that you are capable of such a call called, success. People may tell you that you will never be anything and you are worth nothing. But guess what, their words are merely just a part of a bigger battle than the human eye can perceive.

"For we wrestle not against flesh and blood, but against principalities, against powers, against the rulers of the darkness of this world, against spiritual wickedness in heavenly places." Ephesians 6:12 (NKJV)

The bible lets us know that there is a battle going on in the "heavenly places" which refer to the spirit realm. Why do we have spiritual battles against us? We are 3 part beings - we have a body, a soul and a spirit.

The Soul

Our soul is our rational mind and the place of ourselves that is the storehouse of our sinful desires, emotions, mind and connection to people (which is what we call our heart when we communicate our feelings on things). Our heart is a physical organ, it is not something that is able to do anything by itself. Just think about it, if your heart was transplanted into another person, would that person automatically love your mother or father? No, it is simply just an organ. So, you must know that your soul is the host of sinful desires, mind, emotions and experiences.

"When you follow the desires of your sinful nature, the results are very clear: sexual immorality, impurity, lustful pleasures, idolatry, sorcery, hostility, quarreling, jealousy, outbursts of anger, selfish ambition, dissension, division, envy, drunkenness, wild parties, and other sins like these. Let me tell you again, as I have before, that anyone living that sort of life will not inherit the Kingdom of God." Galatians 5:19-21 (NLT)

"So I say, let the Holy Spirit guide your lives. Then you won't be doing what your sinful nature craves. The sinful nature wants to do evil, which is just the opposite of what the Spirit wants. And the Spirit gives us desires that are the opposite of what the sinful nature desires. These two forces are constantly fighting each other, so you are not free to carry out your good intentions." Galatians 5:17 (NLT)

What is our sinful nature? The desires of the soul. This all came into play after Adam sinned against God in the Garden of Eden. Adam had free will to sin against God or to be obedient, but his soul - which contained his free will, overpowered his desire to please God, and he therefore sinned. This perfectly describes what is discussed in Galatians 5:17. There is literally a war inside you that battles against what you know is right, but you struggle because you want to do what is wrong. This is the battle between living a life of the spirit and the desires of the soul (called the flesh).

Our soul is also affected when we involve ourselves with relationships - whether that be friendships or sexual relationships. **It is very important that we protect our soul from encounters that the word of God considers evil - it is only to protect us, not to limit us.**

Our Spirit

Then we have our spirit which is where God communicates (that gut feeling/something talking to you); but the spirit is also what experiences eternity.

"... and the dust returns to the earth as it was, and the spirit returns to God who gave it." Ecclesiastes 12:7 (KJV)

The spirit is our direct connection to God. When Adam was created, God breathed His spirit into Adam. *"then the Lord God formed the man of dust from the ground and breathed into his nostrils the breath of life, and the man became a living creature."* Genesis 2:7 (ESV) The reference of God breathing His spirit into Adam was from the word "breath" in Hebrew that translates to the word spirit. Since God is a spirit, if we desire to connect with Him, it must be spiritually. We do not connect with God through material objects, rituals or through sacrifices of dead things - we connect with God by His word through allowing Him to be the true leader of our spirit and Healer of our soul. This can only happen by having a relationship with Him spiritually.

"But the Holy Spirit produces this kind of fruit in our lives: love, joy, peace, patience, kindness, goodness, faithfulness, gentleness, and self-control. There is no law against these things!" Galatians 5:22-23 (NLT)

When you walk a life being led by the spirit of God, you will find that God will begin to lead you into a life that produces the fruit of the spirit. I've definitely found myself being stretched in the fruit of patience. All of these "fruits" are character traits that are tested on a daily basis. They are good character traits to have, and they truly reflect who you are as a person whenever you are faced with a circumstance that makes you want to do the opposite. When you exercise these traits, they make you into a powerful human being...but even more so a powerful spirit led being.

Racism

There is also a war against your success, and it's called the spirit of racism. Many people talk about how racism is taught - which is 100% true, but I am going to take this another step further. Knowledge is considered an impartation. To impart something is to give to or to give as an inheritance - think of it as a spiritual transaction. Wisdom is so important because it has the ability to build your soul. In the Bible, we learn that wisdom is imparted (Proverbs 29:15), spiritual gifts are imparted (Romans 1:11) and the Gospel is imparted (1 Thessalonians 2:8). With these things being known, we must understand that where there is good, there is an evil opposite. If we know that wisdom is imparted, there is evil knowledge that can be imparted to people. When racism is imparted in the early stages of childhood, the knowledge of it becomes so ingrained in the child that it becomes their identity - thus, creating a racist.

We must be careful in the way that we raise our children and also aware of the verbiage that we use around them. If you create an atmosphere of hate, disappointment and blame towards a specific race or type of people, your child will inherit that mentality and it will become their identity. Our thoughts dictate our words and our words create our environment. All of these together create your world.

Another thing that we must become aware of is to understand that it is possible to be prejudice against your own race. When you stereotype your ethnicity, calling them degrading names culturally known as racist slurs, and say things like "all (race) people are the same" and other words that degrade your ethnicity - you have become prejudice against your own kind. The root of that truly goes back to self-hatred. Degrading who you are and exalting yourself as though you are not a part of that ethnicity is hating who you truly are and trying to find identity by identifying with another culture/race. How can I say such a thing? I was that person in my middle school years. I was raised watching Barney, raised to talk 'like the Barney girls' because 'talking proper' would land me a job. I was always asked, "why do you talk like a white girl?" I was raised in the suburbs of Georgia. Were many of the people in the suburbs racist? Absolutely, and I wanted to prove that I was different. Because I had been disappointed by african american men and bullied by african americans in school for the many ways I was different - I hated myself. It was self-hatred. But I grew up and I discovered that there was beauty in the skin I was in. The hateful things I heard all throughout school no longer mattered. There was power in being black and there was nothing that could convince me otherwise. I no longer felt like I had to prove racist people wrong - I could be me, unapologetically.

We are Royalty. We must bring awareness of what is taking place in the earth as people target minorities - we must rise up and speak out on injustice. We must take a stance against the enemy that wages war against our race(s) - in the natural and even the more, in the unseen realm.

"For we wrestle not against flesh and blood, but against principalities, against powers, against the rulers of the darkness of this world, against spiritual wickedness in high places." Ephesians 6:12

Desires & Restoration

Our relationship with God is a continuous, growing relationship. And as you go on your journey in your relationship with God, you will notice that He will begin to deal with the desires of your soul, your behavior and characteristics that do not reflect Him.

"Delight yourself in the Lord, and he will give you the desires of your heart." Psalm 37:4 (ESV)

When people read this, they read it as God will give them anything they want. Not true, let's read it in the true context.

The Qualified Life

"The human heart is the most deceitful of all things, and desperately wicked. Who really knows how bad it is ?" Jeremiah 27:9 (NLT)

If the heart is deceitful, why would God give us what our heart wants? We must read 37:4 for what it literally says. GOD WILL GIVE YOU the desires of your heart when you delight yourself in the Lord. There is a divine exchange as you submit your life to the Lord. That divine exchange is God giving you the right desires - which are His desires. And when you are in alignment with His desires, you will automatically experience the blessings of God. **Our own desires and our own understanding leads us onto the path of destruction, but the instruction of the Lord assures us onto the path of fruitfulness.**

You'll also begin to see God bringing light to the places of our souls that need healing from any bad experiences, hurt, trauma. This definitely includes dealing with your soul experiences through sexual encounters outside of marriage, emotions and anything that we have involved ourselves with that goes against the will/word of God. Any relationship that has had an effect on your soul, God will bring the mirror of His word to show you how He feels about it so that you can become more like Him. Some of these things may be painful to look back at, but He brings it to light so that He can be your Healer and the One that you run to for restoration. I've seen God do this in my life as I have gone through the pain of a dissolved marriage. He has rebuilt me and has restored my confidence. It took time in His presence, prayer, many days crying, multiple counseling sessions and most importantly - being honest with myself and my feelings.

Living a life that is led by the spirit is the life that is more fulfilling than winging life day by day. When we don't live a life of walking with God, we easily numb ourselves to our hurts and try to forget about trauma through addictions or other dependencies. But when you walk with God, He exposes those things to bring you into a whole life - a life that helps you to walk in your success, qualified. God doesn't want you to live "successful" in pain and fragmented. He wants you healed. The war over your success is simply put: the enemy wants you to live a life walking in your own desires and a life that is not whole or healed. The enemy wants you to pursue a success that is temporary while you are not healed or whole. If any evil spirits can influence you to lose your peace of mind and walk into a life of rebellion against the will of God (through living out your own definition of success) you are not a threat against the rulers of darkness. We are designed to defeat the powers of darkness through dominion in walking with God. And you can't defeat your spiritual enemies if you are not walking with God or in the ways of God. The agenda of hell is to make you think that success is attained outside of God. And if you find your success outside of God's will, then God cannot bless you in fullness and you will not experience Heaven on Earth.

Notes

The Qualified Life

Chapter 9: Limitless Confidence

How often have you said, "I have low self-esteem"? My question to you is, why? Who told you that?

Your confidence has nothing to do with other people's actions. Why allow someone to disqualify you and make you feel as though you have no confidence?

No one should be given the right to strip you from your confidence.

Your confidence was never meant to be placed in man - it was meant to be placed in the truth and God! There are various areas that we need to address our confidence and remain firm in those areas, which includes our faith in God, where we stand with God (eternity), the state of our heart and your confidence in His word.

Where do you stand in your faith in God? Have you received from Him since you believed? I know that when we go through trials or loss it is easy to lose faith, but God is good despite our disappointments. There are times you may not understand His sovereignty, but He promises that He will *never fail us, leave us nor forsake us,* according to Hebrews 13:5 (NIV, MSG). We cannot be moved in our faith because things don't go our way - for *we walk by faith and not by sight* (2 Corinthians 5:7). I encourage you, take hold of the justification that we have in Christ (Romans 1:5) which means to live with a clean slate as though our sins never happened! You are a new creation through Christ (2 Corinthians 5:17).

Hebrews 4:16 in the NIV translation tells us, *"Let us then approach God's throne of grace with confidence, so that we may receive mercy and find grace to help us in our time of need."*. This is a scripture that can assure us that God is approachable. Why should we think that we do not have access to God and that He would strike us dead if we dare come near Him? His word tells us that we can approach His throne of grace (which is attaining that which you did not earn) and approaching Him with confidence so that you can receive mercy and grace! This is not telling us to continue in our sin (Romans 6:1-2), however it tells us that we can approach God without condemnation.

"What shall we then say to these things? If God be for us, who can be against us?" Romans 8:31 (KJV)

As far as the state of our heart, it is imperative that we guard our mind and our heart's from the lies and deceptions of the enemy.

"Guard your heart above all else, for it determines the course of your life." Proverbs 4:23 (NLT)

"Do not conform to the pattern of this world, but be transformed by the renewing of your mind. Then you will be able to test and approve what God's will is—his good, pleasing and perfect will." Romans 12:2 (NIV)

The scriptures let us know that we must guard our heart and to renew our mind's daily. What does this mean? Let go of the way that you once thought; let go of the memories of people belittling you and telling you that you weren't good enough. I am here to let you know, you are qualified to live a qualified life!

Living a qualified life isn't about people suddenly coming into the understanding of who you are and giving you tremendous amounts of favor - that's just a perk. However, living the qualified life is about you understanding that you have a place. It's all about discovering who you are, Whose you are, why you are here, where you are going and what work there is to be done while you are living your time on this earth. It's not about acceptance from man, it's about accepting yourself. When you accept your life's purpose and who you are made to be, everything begins to fall in place for you.

Your confidence should never be in the hands of man, because man will fail you. If man will fail you, man has the potential to drop you. No person is perfect, but your confidence should solely be in the hands of God. When God has your heart in His hand and you are completely His, you will discover that *doors will be opened to you that no man can shut* (Revelations 3:8). The **key** to The Qualified Life is allowing God to be the sovereign one of your life and your purpose on earth. He is the One that holds the keys to all of your opportunities. Your promotion is through and in God - not you. Your gift will make room for you, but the key is in the hands of the Lord.

"For promotion cometh neither from the east, nor from the west, nor from the south. But God is the judge: he putteth down one, and setteth up another." Psalm 74:6-7 (KJV)

The one thing that will make you stand out in this world is living a life that is led by the spirit of God. When you live by the leading of the Lord, you will walk a path of success beyond others. People live in chaos because they have chosen to live outside the grace and direction of God. We can try to do it on our own - and lack peace because we don't know the ending. However, when we choose to

The Qualified Life

walk with God, we walk in peace (even when hell is breaking loose) because His word tells us that He will never leave us. *Even through the fire, He is with us.* In the past, I experienced being on a mental breakdown because I tried to handle things way beyond me, in my own strength. But, it was when I decided to abide in the Lord, I had the grace, the ability to move forward with an anticipated hope.

So, what about you? Are you going to decide to live the Qualified life that God has planned out for you since the very beginning, or are you going to choose to allow Him to be the Sovereign One of your life's decisions. Your qualification is in the hands of God. He promised you a hope and a future, and it is in that future that you are qualified to walk in the realm of influence that you were purposed to walk in. We are nothing without Him, and without Him - we have nothing, because He is everything. When you walk with God, you will have everything you need and you will advance into new heights. He is the key to all things. This is, The Qualified Life.

Chapter 10 - Your Next Chapter

After reading this book, it's time to apply what you've learned throughout this journey. There were many statements that were made that makes you ponder on what steps you need to make in order to walk into this next level of your life. So, this chapter belongs to you. 10, for completion. I am giving these next few pages for you to write affirmations, write scriptures, goals and steps you can take to walk in the direction that God has ordered for you. Take time to reflect, quiet yourself and listen to what God has to say. You may hear a simple sentence, you may hear a word…or you may get an idea. God may even tell you some things that He wants to heal within you during this time of your life. Whatever these things may be, these pages are for you to open your heart and heal. Open your heart and write vision. This is "your next chapter". Consider this your new beginning. Consider this your first step into a life of healing and divine instruction from your Creator. Embrace it, write and run with what God has in store for you - because you are Qualified!

The Qualified Life

For more from Veonne Anderson

Visit www.VeonneAnderson.com for products,

booking and services.

The Qualified Life

References

- "Greek Lexicon :: (KJV)."Terminology for Greek and Hebrew terminology Blue Letter Bible. Web.<http://www.blueletterbible.org/lang/lexicon/>.

- NIV References - Holy Bible: New International Version. Grand

Rapids, MI: Zondervan, 2011. Print.

- GWT References - Holy Bible: New International Version.

Grand Rapids, MI: Zondervan, 2011. Print.

- NLT References - Holy Bible: New Living Translation.

Wheaton, IL: Tyndale House, 1996. Print.

- ESV Text Edition: 2011"Scripture quotations are from The Holy Bible,

English Standard Version® (ESV®), copyright © 2001 by Crossway,

a publishing ministry of Good News Publishers. Used by permission.

All rights reserved."

- AMP References - The Holy Bible: Amplified Version. Grand

Rapids, MI: Zondervan Pub. House, 1987. Print.

www.ingramcontent.com/pod-product-compliance
Lightning Source LLC
Chambersburg PA
CBHW070041100426
42740CB00013B/2752